A Glimpse of Indian Railways, 1975

Compiled by Colin Stone
Images by Brian Walker

© Images and Design: The Transport Treasury 2022. Text: Colin Stone

ISBN 978-1-913893-19-4

First published in 2022 by Transport Treasury Publishing Ltd. 16 Highworth Close, High Wycombe, HP13 7PJ
Totem Publishing, an imprint of Transport Treasury Publishing.

www.ttpublishing.co.uk

Printed in Tarxien, Malta By Gutenberg Press Ltd.

'A Glimpse of Indian Railways, 1975' is one of a series of books on specialist transport subjects published in strictly limited numbers and produced under the Totem Publishing imprint using material only available at The Transport Treasury.

Bibliography:
Indian Narrow Gauge Railways by Hugh Hughes and Frank Jux, published independently circa 1968.
The Indian Railway Fan Club website, which includes a paper by R.R. Bandari.
Wikipedia.
However the majority of information has come from my 1975 tour notebook, with additional material from 46-year-old memories, thus any errors are solely my responsibility. C. Stone, May 2021.

Front cover: Indian Narrow Gauge had a charm all of its own. That charm is demonstrated here in a scene most would associate with an Indian train, that of passengers clinging to the side of a packed service. An isolated 39 miles long 2ft 6 inch gauge line ran from Ankleswar to Rajpipla, off that route was a 19 mile long branch. In this view, Class W1 0-6-4 No 592 departs Ankleswar at 09.00 with the one and only daily through train to the branch terminus at Netrang. Four Class W1 0-6-4's were built by Bagnall in 1948 as the final development of the Class W which can be seen elsewhere in this volume.

Frontis piece: After a day acclimatising most of the group travelled the 11 miles out of Bombay (Mumbai) to the suburb of Andheri. Having ridden in one of the ubiquitous suburban e.m.u's, such as set No 69 seen here, we followed Indian practice and wandered off the end of the platform to take up position for line side photography. Note the general populace wandering at will along the tracks, when in urban areas we soon learnt that trying to obtain photographs without extraneous persons in view was futile.
9 November 1975

Rear cover: More Indian narrow gauge railway charm, in this view a 2 foot 6 inch gauge Class ZB 2-6-2 No 79 built by Krauss-Maffei in 1952 departs Dabhoi with freight. The British influence on Indian Railways is apparent from the signals and "clean" lines of the loco'. Whilst the lady and daughter sun drying the "cow pats" they have collected and compressed by hand to burn as domestic fuel, is pure India.

Introduction

"Mighty Oaks from Little Acorns grow", most likely not a thought that crossed the mind of the late William "Bill" Alborough when he ran his first tour to Switzerland in 1971. By the advent of Bill's second venture across the English Channel the title "To Europe For Steam" (TEFS) had been bestowed on his new concern. TEFS, as the title suggests, provided travel itineraries for railway enthusiasts with a predominant interest in steam, but at a leisurely pace. This meant hotels at night rather than "dossing" on platforms or trains, and meals consisting of more than a bag of crisps and a bottle of beer. This step up from the bare bones of some rail tours saw TEFS eventually attract a regular band of participants including ladies i.e. wives and girl friends. As this clientele returned time and time again to travel with TEFS, Bill Alborough had obviously "got it right". Friendships forged during those tours endured for many years, in many a wistful reminiscence, those jaunts were, and still are, fondly remembered. Breaking out of Europe in 1974 with an epic South African tour, TEFS then became known as "To Everywhere For Steam".

In November 1975, India was added to the growing number of countries on the TEFS "everywhere" list. It wasn't the first visit to the sub continent by a group of British railway enthusiasts, nor would it be the last. However, as most participants were already well acquainted with one another, it was perhaps one of the most convivial and fun filled tours. Of only sixteen days duration, just a small part of that vast country and its railway system could be visited, but good planning meant the group saw a diverse cross section of India and its people. Rail travel over all four of the main gauges then extant in India was achieved to some degree. These being Broad (5 foot 6 inches, often referred to as Indian Gauge), Metre, 2 foot 6 inches and twofoot gauges. Add in motive power depot visits, line side photography, footplate rides and a visit to a well known, awesome tourist venue, it was no wonder the tour was oversubscribed.

As a group, although we visited India, it is probably fairer to say we "experienced" India. Nothing really prepared us for what we saw, smelt, endured, but above all enjoyed about India. Endured? ... Unfortunately most of the group suffered at some stage from the old music hall joke of "Delhi Belly", but not enough to ruin the whole adventure. Indian way of life, contrasts in living and working conditions seen across the country were somewhat alien to our western eyes. The railway system, as an employer of a vast number of the Indian population, was a microcosm of the country itself. A lot of Indian railway practice was so very familiar, but some working conditions we saw were viewed with much incredulity. Wherever we went on Indian Railway property we were greeted courteously and with great friendliness by all levels and grades of staff and this welcoming attitude applied throughout India as a whole.

On the locomotive front what could be loosely called Indian "standard steam types" formed the majority of what was seen, but several older classes were also noted. In the early 1950s Indian Railways were "zoned" such as Central Railway (CR), Northeast Frontier (NF) and so on. Around the same time there was a loose attempt at locomotive identification, such as P and G for Passenger and Goods. Broad Gauge types were prefixed W for wide, or with a Y for Metre Gauge locomotives. However, to confuse matters, several pre 1950 forms of identification were still in use in 1975. Of the individual steam locomotive types/classes seen during the tour, all are represented by at least one image in this album. Just six images contain a "modern traction" element, these are included to illustrate the changes being introduced which eventually caused the demise of steam. Regular working steam on Indian Railways lasted until December 1995 on Broad Gauge, and until circa 1998 on Metre Gauge. Images selected follow the tour itinerary across India beginning in Bombay, now known as Mumbai. Thus for the book I have used location names in use at the time of the visit, any new appellation, where known, is bracketed in the first instance only. Caption information primarily covers the 1975 tour, but in 1990 Indian Railways embarked on "Project Uni-Gauge", a scheme to standardise as many routes as possible to 5 foot 6 inch gauge. Thus, where known the current status of some of the routes visited have been included for the sake of interest.

Photographs for this album were taken by the late Brian Walker, a regular participant on TEFS tours. Brian Walker resided in Burton Joyce on the outskirts of Nottingham; a career railwayman, he started life on British Railways (BR) straight from school, eventually becoming a signalman in the Colwick area. Following closure of his signal box he was moved from job to job within BR, including being a shunter at Nottingham Carriage sidings. Latterly he became a member of Nottingham station staff. Brian retired from a position of leading railwayman due to ill health in the late 1990s. Meeting Brian on a TEFS tour to Germany in 1972 we became firm friends and later organised several of our own personal tours to Germany and South Africa. Following Brian's death in 2014 his slide collection passed to Trevor Davis, another TEFS regular, they can be viewed in full on the Transport Treasury website within the Trevor Davis Gallery.

Colin Stone, Poole, Dorset. October 2021.

Added for your persual/amusement "The Happy Band" 46 years in 1975, my guess is, sadly not many still survive? A scan of a print found in my archive!

Broad Gauge WP Pacific No 7466 of the Western Railway is captured at the head of the "Flying Ranee" nearing the end of its journey from Surat to Bombay Central station. Although No 7466 is one of 300 WP's built in 1949 in the USA and Canada, its actual builder is unknown due to an early system error of issuing running numbers in blocks without cross referencing to builders details. Class lettering indicates W for Wide i.e. Broad Gauge and P for Passenger.
9 November 1975

Later in the day, in another Bombay suburb, two Western Railway ex USATC Class WD 2-8-2's double head a freight over Mahim Creek. Although in theory identical, the lead locomotive No 12449 is classified AWD due to it being built in America (A) by Baldwin in 1944. Whilst No 12644 is classed as CWD, being a 1946 product of the Canadian Locomotive Company (C).
9 November 1975

Two Class WDS1 Bo-Bo diesel shunters cross Mahim Creek light engine, No 19014 leads No 19008. These 1944 built, 385 h.p. General Electric products were the first diesels to run in India, 50 were brought over by the United States Army Transportation Corps (USATC) for use in the ports of Bombay, Calcutta (Kolkata) and Karachi during WW2. Fifteen remained in India following the 1947 partition, the last Indian example saw use in 1992, one is preserved.
9 November 1975

WP Pacific No 7546 built 1955 by Canadian Locomotive Company nears the end of its journey as it crosses Mahim Creek. The fellow just visible squatting on the bridge pipe work, to the right, was dubbed "River Man" by the group. Various items, including coins, were often thrown off passing trains for "River Man" to try and retrieve by diving into the creek. His assistant, in the blue shirt, collected anything that landed on the bridge decking.
9 November 1975

A visit to the 2 foot gauge Matheran Light Railway (MLR) was the first scheduled event for the whole group. An early morning, 62 mile rail journey by broad gauge electric would take us to Neral, where on arrival MLR Class ML 0-6-0T locomotive No 740 was in action in the narrow gauge yard, CR on the side tank indicates the MLR is part of the Central Railway subdivision of Indian Railways. Built in Germany in 1907 by Orenstein & Koppel No 740 now resides in the UK, originally based on the Leighton Buzzard Railway it later moved north to the South Tynedale Railway.
10 November 1975

Although the British developed Matheran as a hill station, the connecting MLR was proposed and constructed by Indians. Promoted by Abdul Hussein Peerbhoy, the project was financed by his father Sir Adamjee Peerbhoy. Opened in 1907 the 13 mile line climbs on fierce gradients, some as steep as 1 in 20, to 2,625 feet above sea level at the Matheran terminus. With Class ML 0-6-0T No 738 in charge the group travelled up the line. Although on board a regular service train, several false starts and run pasts were staged for the group, as witnessed here. As the first locomotive delivered to the line from Orenstein & Koppel in 1905, No 738 is now plinthed at Neral station.
10 November 1975

As well as steep gradients, the locos also faced very sharp curves, as severe as 60ft radius in places. Although built by Orenstein & Koppel, the engines were designed by the MLR's British consulting engineer Everard Calthrop who had them fitted with the Klien-Lindner system of articulation. This system was a close development of Sir Arthur Heywood's 1881 ingenious design of radiating axle first used on his Duffield Bank Railway. In this view MLR No 738 sits on one of the curves during another of the impromptu photographic stops made during the ascent. 10 November 1975

Diesels first arrived on the MLR in 1956 when four Class NDM-1's were delivered from Arnold Jung of Germany. Seen here departing Neral with a morning service is No 502 of that batch. With the influx of more diesels, steam was finally ousted from the line in 1982. However all four of the steam fleet are preserved, No's 738 & 740 as previously noted, with No 741 plinthed at Matheran and No 739 in the Indian National Railway Museum, New Delhi.
10 November 1975

Industrial steam was noted during a scheduled visit to the Bombay Port Trust's Wadala depot. Here the group had the pleasure of seeing Class A 2-6-0T No 15 trundling sedately through the depot yard. One of 30 of the type acquired by the port between 1913 and 1922, this example was the first of a final batch of ten built by Nasmyth Wilson in 1921.
11 November 1975

Also on view at Wadala were the Class H 2-10-2 tank engines. Just two of these substantial, weighty machines were built in 1922 by Nasmyth Wilson. No 25H is seen in this view with the bunker of the other, No 26H just visible left. Listed as hump shunters in one set of records, whatever their tasks it is doubtful if either of them worked again as both locomotives were stored in a siding.
11 November 1975

An internal flight took us to Gujarat state for time in the Cities of Ahmedabad and Baroda (Vadadora), where the group had a first sight of Indian Metre gauge steam. In this view YP 4-6-2 No 2171 makes a surefooted start away from Ahmedabad Junction station. From a Class total of 871, this example built in 1954 was one of 200 YP's built in Germany by Krauss-Maffei. Note left, the amount of onlookers that we as westerners attracted. Even the mundane task of changing film drew a curious audience, but at no time did we ever feel threatened in any way.
12 November 1975

Another view at Ahmedabad which symbolises the eventual fate of Indian steam, here a diesel, built in 1968 by Montreal Locomotive Works, No 6266 of Class YDM4A is in the foreground. Whilst, what appears to be a Class YB steam locomotive, is seen in the distance. Although diesel and electric traction would steadily push steam further into the background, it would take around another 20 years before final extinction.
12 November 1975

Located on the northern outskirts of Ahmedabad was Sabarmati metre gauge MPD. Some sheds were utter tips, Sabarmati was one of the better ones, witness the wording above the shed entrance which appears to be cleaned regularly. Posed outside is Class YB 4-6-2 No 30041, one of a batch built by Robert, Stephenson & Hawthorn in 1949. Production of the type began in 1927 continuing in batches until 1951. Some 50 examples were also sold directly to Burma Railways.
12 November 1975

Sabarmati shed pilot was this sturdy, elegant looking Class D2 4-6-4T No 331. Built in India at the Ajmer Locomotive Works in 1928 it was one of 25 built for the Bombay, Baroda & Central India Railway. It is seen brewing up in the shed yard. This and sister engine No 334, also on shed, were the only two of the type noted, neither received a number under the all India locomotive renumbering scheme. It is tempting to suggest that Whitelegg's Glasgow & South Western Railway Baltic Tanks had an influence on the design?
12 November 1975

A study of Class YL 2-6-2 No 5193 at Sabarmati receiving attention to its left hand steam pipe, note the steam pipe cover resting on the running plate. Built for mixed traffic and branch line use, it had a light axle load of 8 tons. One of 264 built, this example was constructed in Hungary by Mavag of Budapest in 1957.
12 November 1975

Class YD 2-8-2 No 30206 stands in Sabarmati shed yard in Western Railway plain black livery. Primarily for main line freight use, these locos had a 10 ton axle load, 171 of the type were built, 61 for use in Burma (Myanmar), 25 for East Pakistan (Bangladesh). Of the 85 Indian based examples, this one was home built in 1934 by the Ajmer Locomotive works.
12 November 1975

Two Class YG 2-8-2's are caught side by side at the rear of Sabarmati shed, a total of 1,074 of the type were built by various manufactures. On the left, No 4032 without smoke deflectors of 1954 vintage, came from Nippon Sharyo, Japan. Whilst on the right No 4132, with deflectors, was constructed in Czechoslovakia by Lenin-Werke (Skoda) in 1956.
12 November 1975

Close to Sabarmati depot was Kali Road station, nearing the end of its 85 mile journey, Class YB 4-6-2 No 30012, built 1935 in India by Ajmer Locomotive Works is seen approaching with the 04.50 Taranga Hill to Ahmedabad service.
12 November 1975

A Class B2 4-6-0 No 31028 sends up a fine plume of black smoke as it prepares to leave Sabarmati station with a local passenger service. Group members Bob Francis, Terry Velvick and Colin Harrison capture it and the antics of its happy band of gesticulating passengers on film. Robert Stephenson & Hawthorn built the locomotive in 1950.
12 November 1975

Three languages Hindi, Gujurati and English on the running in board proclaim to all passengers they are arriving at Sabarmati. In this instance these passengers are less flamboyant, Class YP 4-6-2 No 2472 built 1952 in Glasgow by North British clanks its way sedately in for its station stop.
12 November 1975

Class YP 4-6-2 No 2481 stands at Dangarwa station at the head of a train from Ahmedabad. This 1952 built North British product took the group the 41 miles from Sabarmati to Mahesana and provided some with their first footplate trip of the tour. Our camera man has just left the footplate, while the crew wait for him to re-board the train, a feral dog waits expectantly for a titbit of food. Like most of the Indian metre gauge network this route has been converted to Broad gauge.
12 November 1975

Having seen a B2 4-6-0 in action earlier, Mahesana Junction depot provided closer inspection of the type. Vulcan Foundry turned out No 31035 in 1947 as one of four built for the Gondal Railway, in 1951 all four became part of the Western Railway division of Indian Railways.
12 November 1975

Looking like suitable motive power for Arnold Ridley's Ghost Train, this Class YF 2-6-2 No 30321, built in 1937 by Ajmer, had been involved in a "roll over" derailment. Having been extracted from the creek it landed in, it was dumped in its new livery of dried mud and rust at the rear of Mahesana Junction shed, never to run again. The original YF's were built as 0-6-2 tank engines with a light 8 ton axle load for branch line duties. They proved to be unstable, thus some were rebuilt as 2-6-2's. However, a final batch of 25, including No 30321, were built as straight 2-6-2's.
12 November 1975

This heavily cannibalised Class YF 2-6-2 No 30323 (Ajmer 1937) awaits a fate similar to that of its white sister, a one way trip to the scrap yard. Of 25 built as 2-6-2's, the first 15 had Rotary Cam poppet valve gear, as seen here, the YF type eventually totalled 111. Just five examples were noted in 1975, all dumped out of use at Mahesana, and all from the Rotary Cam group.
12 November 1975

The visit to Mahesana Junction MPD allowed this portrait shot of Class YG 2-8-2 No 4380 to be taken as it arrived on shed after a day's duty. Tata Engineering and Locomotive Company (TELCO) produced this one on home soil in 1959. Eventually totalling 1,074 locomotives built in the period 1949 to 1972, the latter year saw No 3573 of the type claim the sad honour of being the last main line steam locomotive built in India for Indian Railways.
12 November 1975

A small piece of Indian Railway practice is viewed here. Long before the age of data storage on computers, the cab side of Class YG No 4380 carries a wealth of information about the locomotive. The assumption being you'd have a hard job to lose all that information having painted it on the side, as well as saving time looking for the appropriate record card! 12 November 1975

Class YP 4-6-2 No 2090, another Telco product dating from 1954, was quite vocal as it got a lengthy passenger train away from Mahesana station on the main line adjacent to the MPD.
12 November 1975

Coaling a locomotive Indian style at Mahesana Junction. In a country where shortage of labour was no problem, manual coaling was commonplace. In this view Class B2 4-6-0 No 31018 is being tended to by a gang of eight men. Two men shovel coal into metal pans, two other lads lift the pans onto the heads off four chaps who then ascend ladders and tip the coal into the loco tender. The same procedure is often carried out on the other side simultaneously, at Mahesana two locos could be dealt with from three separate coal piles. The two gents in white are overseers.
12 November 1975, *Colin Stone*

Competing motive power at Mahesana. A YP Pacific moves a rake of passenger coaches around the yard while a 1968 built Class YDM4A diesel No 6206 heads a freight along the main line. India was by now building its own diesels, this loco came from the aptly named Diesel Locomotive Works (DLW) based in Varanasi. Following gauge conversion several of the type were sold to overseas metre gauge railways.
12 November 1975

In this final view at Mahesana Junction MPD a small array of Indian Metre gauge steam is lined up for the camera, it comprises Left to Right :- B2 31018, YB 30022, YP 2803 and YP 2443.
12 November 1975

Another day, another gauge, a bus ride south from Baroda took us to Nadiad 2 foot 6 inch gauge depot. On arrival we found this 1925 built Bagnall Class WT 0-6-4T, No 597 posed for us on a 45 foot turntable built by Ormerod & Grierson, Hulme, Manchester. With a build date of 1874 it was a transplant from elsewhere as the line here didn't open until 1914. It wasn't clear if No 597 was the "depot pet", or if it had been cleaned and adorned with headboard etc' especially for our visit.
13 November 1975

Once the WT had been photographed it moved off to be prepared for its allotted duty. Its place was taken by Class ZB 2-6-2 No 117 built 1959 in Yugoslavia by Duro Dakovic, Industrija Lokomotiva, Strojeva i Mostova, Slavonski Brod, this was usually shortened to SlBr (I can't think why !), The shed master can be seen on the footplate along with an elderly driver who moved the locos around for us.
13 November 1975

Two routes emanated from Nadaid, to Kapadvanj (28 miles, opened 1913) and to Bhadran (36 miles, opened 1914). Surpringly they weren't physically connected until 1953. With the system isolated from the main 2 foot 6 inch network, the depot undertook minor repairs to its stud of around 10 locomotives. In this view another 1925 built Bagnall Class WT 0-6-4T, No 599 receives attention to its driving wheel axle boxes.
13 November 1975

After earlier shed photography, Class WT No 597 was booked to work the 09.10 Nadiad to Petlad Junction situated 22 miles down the Bhadran line. Joining the train or the locomotive footplate, the group travelled the first 12 miles to Sojitra, a crossing point on the line. Having stopped short, No 597 prepares to run past a line up of cameras into Sojitra station.
13 November 1975

Sojitra crossing point sees Class ZB 2-6-2 No 120 arrive with a service for Nadiad. Built in 1959 by SIBr, No 120 was from the last batch of Indian Railway Standard design (IRS) narrow gauge steam locomotives to be delivered to Indian Railways. Of the 12 built, 6 went to the Western Railway sub division, the remainder going to an independent irrigation project. The Bhadran route had an average four trains per day in 1975, but was down to one return working by 2017. Reports suggest it closed that year due to monsoon washouts of track and bridges. Since then part of the route has reopened following gauge conversion to 5 foot 6 inch.
13 November 1975

In this view a Class WL (L for Light) 4-6-2 arrives into Petlad Junction. Built at Chittaranjan works in 1966 primarily for working secondary routes and branch lines, No 15040 is doing just that on the 33 mile branch from Anand Junction to Khambhat. Of note, a sister WL worked the last scheduled steam hauled Indian Railways broad gauge service in November 1995. A Class WG No 8198 is visible in the background.
13 November 1975

Anand Junction MPD, This portrait of Class WG 2-8-2 No 9582, home built at Chittaranjan works in 1957 shows India's most numerous type of broad gauge steam locomotive. From 1950, 2,450 examples were built in eight countries, in 1970 a WG, No 10560, was the last Broad Gauge steam loco' to be built in India, it was suitably named "Antim Sitara" (Last Star). Nine WG's survive in preservation.
13 November 1975

The incredible sight of ladies coaling locomotives greeted us at Anand. Forget the saying "The Weaker Sex", think more "Girl Power" when you notice that the ladies are doing the job bare foot! Note the protective pads on top of their heads providing the bare minimum of head protection, also note the young girl toddler in the coal truck with just lumps of coal to play with, an extreme example of on the job training?
13 November 1975, *Colin Stone*

The next port of call was Baroda broad gauge depot where this elegant Class H 4-6-0 No 24296 was spotted in the yard. To overcome haphazard Indian locomotive development a series of designs by the British Engineering Standard Association (BESA) was conceived in 1905 and held sway until 1928. This 1922 North British built loco' is one such. When viewing this immaculate locomotive, which is obviously its drivers pride and joy, I recall the comments of a Society programme organiser when offered a slide show on India Railways. "We don't want any of that foreign rubbish" ...Rubbish! ...Really?
13 November 1975.

Having seen hand coaling of engines at Mahesana and Anand, this sight at Baroda showed coaling at a mechanised level. Here a steam crane of British origins is seen in action filling the tender of a another Class H 4-6-0, in this instance No 24313, one of a batch of 25 constructed by William Beardmore & Co in 1923 for the Bombay, Baroda and Central India Railway.
13 November 1975.

The delights of Indian narrow gauge, and where better to see it than Dhaboi, the centre of what was once the Gaekwar of Baroda's State Railway. Five 2 foot 6 inch gauge routes, including branch lines radiated from Dhaboi, totalling some 320 miles. At the time of our visit about 40 locomotives where allocated to the system. Most of the older locomotives still in use were relegated to light duties such as this Class C 2-8-4T No 560, one of three built by Kerr Stuart in 1921. 14 November 1975.

This Class P 4-6-0 No 607, seen moving a short trip freight along the main line adjacent to Dhaboi motive power depot, is not as old as it looks. Bagnall produced two locomotives in 1949 replicating a 1929 design which also comprised two locos, both the 1949 built examples were at Dabhoi on the day of the group visit.
14 November 1975

"Patience is virtue" was a lesson learnt in India, almost invariably on entering most Motive Power Depots tea was offered as a polite welcoming gesture. Thus regardless of what locomotive "goodies" awaited the camera lens, it was a politeness on our behalf to accept the offer. As Mr Mohinder Singh the Chief Mechanical engineer for the area decided he would meet our group during the Dabhoi depot visit, the staff there pulled out all the stops. Tables, with cloths adorned with floral decoration, plus office seats were set out on the veranda of the foreman's office. Mr Singh invited tour organiser, the late Bill Alborough, to join him for tea and biscuits. Both are seen here along with some of the ladies from the group, who had been garlanded with flowers on arrival at the depot.

14 November 1975, *Colin Stone*

No doubt to curry favour with Mr Singh (no pun intended!) Dabhoi shed staff had Class ZB 2-8-2 No 98 built 1953 by Krauss-Maffei especially cleaned, painted and adorned with brass decorations on the smoke box and buffer beam. After tea, in a surprise move, No 98 was ceremoniously driven out from under cover into the yard, where Mr Mohinder Singh was invited to name the engine after himself. No 98 then did a few shunts up and down the shed yard with group members on the footplate.
14 November 1975

Dating from 1912 this Hudswell, Clarke Class B 2-8-4T No 0557 was showing her age as she wheezed her way around Dabhoi station performing pilot duties. It seems as though her front pony truck has been removed into the bargain? Only six of the type, all for the Bombay, Baroda and Central India Railway were built, three examples were noted at Dabhoi.
14 November 1975

Departing Dabhoi by road coach gave opportunity for some line side photography. French built Class ZB 2-8-2 No 73 a product of Corpet, Louvet in 1958, had been noted being prepared on shed earlier. Heading for Pratapnagar (Baroda), she was soon overtaken and caught on film galloping along in fine style at the head of a mixed train. The engine crew having spotted us leaping from the bus, obliged by providing a burst of black smoke and a long whistle blast. 14 November 1975

Reaching the village of Kelanpur we found another mixed train heading from Pratapnagar to Dabhoi. Posed nicely in the sun, flanked by trees on both sides, Class ZB 2-8-2 No 68 (Bagnall 1952), presented a not to be missed photo' opportunity. As she waited patiently for sister locomotive No 73 to arrive off the single line from Dabhoi, life in India, away from the cities, continued at a slower pace around her.
14 November 1975

"Knock three times and ask for Q". Not quite as melodramatic as a Bond film, but our instructions were to be at the gate by "X hour" and she'll be brought out to you. The "she" in question was this sole example of Class K 2-6-4T built by Kerr Stuart in 1928 for the isolated 9 ½ mile long Piplod to Devgad Baria line. By 1975 No 563 was employed as works shunter at Pratapnagar, located on the outskirts of Baroda. Security issues precluded a group visit to the works, so at the appointed hour the gate opened, No 563 appeared, had her 5 minutes of glory, then disappeared back whence she came.
14 November 1975

An evening stroll from hotel to Baroda broad gauge station allowed a photo' or two of Indian overhead electric locomotives. Indian Railways first electric trains ran in Bombay in 1925 on a 1,500 Volt DC system. In 1961 India adopted the international standard of 25KV AC for all its railways. This Class WCAM1 Co-Co No 21800, bringing a splash of colour to the scene in its new livery, was just two years old. It was the first of a production run of 54 dual voltage, mixed traffic locomotives turned out of Chittaranjan works. As such it had two pantographs, one for each voltage, in this view it is in 25KV mode. Following complete conversion of the Western Railway division to 25KV in 2015, all of the class were withdrawn.
14 November 1975

Ankleswar, 52 miles south of Baroda was the start point of a 39 mile, 2 foot 6 inch gauge line to Rajpipla, there was also a 19 mile long branch line off this route. In this view a 1938 built Bagnall Class W 0-6-4, No 587 leaves Ankleswar with the morning Rajpipla service. Once part of the Gaekwar of Baroda's State Railway (GBSR) this totally isolated mini system saw the branch close in 1995 and the main route converted to 5 foot 6 inch gauge in 2014.
15 November 1975

Class W 0-6-4 No 572, at the head of the 09.35 Kosamba to Umarpada service is one of six built by Bagnall in 1912, eventually the type totalled 22 locomotives. It is seen here arriving at a wayside halt (possibly Limbara), having got us to the halt for a line side photograph, the tour bus decided to expire. Waving the green flag from the footplate is our Indian guide returning with news a replacement rescue bus was on its way. Situated around 12 miles south of Ankleswar, this 37 mile line was another isolated section of the GBSR 2 foot 6 inch gauge network, it too is listed for gauge conversion to 5ft 6".
15 November 1975

An overnight train journey took the group 615 miles north from Baroda to Delhi. With 80 miles of our journey still to go, the lovely low light of a cold dawn illuminates Class CWD 2-8-2 No 12535 as it thumps its freight train into the yard at Mathura Junction. Canadian Locomotive Company, Montreal built the locomotive for the USATC in 1944.
16 November 1975

Originally for working suburban passenger trains this chunky 0-6-2T of Class WW, No 15012 had been relegated to shed pilot duties at Delhi Junction MPD. One of four built in 1940 at Newton-le-Willows by Vulcan Foundry, it was the only one seen during the tour. Visible in the foreground is an example of the abject poverty that could be found in India. A family of three, father, mother and son squat by the locomotive sifting through the ashes thrown from fireboxes in the hope of finding any un-burnt coal for their own domestic use.
16 November 1975, *Colin Stone*

Wearing the blue and white livery of the Central Railway, Class WP 4-6-2 No 7733 forges across Tilak Bridge on the outskirts of Delhi with the 15.45 New Delhi to Agra service. No 7733, built in 1967 at Chittaranjan Works, was one of the last batch of 30 of the type to be built. None of the 755 WP's were constructed in the UK, with their 5 foot 7 inch diameter driving wheels they were India's principal broad gauge express steam locomotive and capable of 70 mph, 9 are preserved.
16 November 1975

Approaching Tilak Bridge this Class WG 2-8-2 No 8013 built by Chittaranjan Locomotive Works in 1959 is illuminated to perfection by the setting sun. Although the G in WG stands for Goods, in this instance No 8013 was doing a good impression of a passenger engine. With 15 coaches in tow bound for Delhi she was rattling along at cracking pace.
16 November 1975

A road coach journey saw the group head 130 miles south from Delhi to the state of Uttar Pradesh and the City of Agra. Arrival was just in time to capture passing WP's, No 7733 departing (left) was returning to Delhi, as sister No 7574 (Canadian Locomotive Co, 1955) arrived on the "Taj Express". The name of the express is a clue to main purpose of the trip to Agra, this was a visit to the awe inspiring Taj Mahal. The entire group, even the most hardened gricer agreed it was well worth the effort.
17 November 1975

Before forsaking steam for culture, Agra depot yielded another locomotive type to the camera. Here 1931 built Class XA1 4-6-2 No 22054 was captured taking water, note the sliding chimney cover, a feature not seen on other classes. Built in three batches by Vulcan Foundry, a total of 113 were constructed with a 13 ton axle load for branch line passenger work. After partition, 76 remained in India, two are preserved, the prefix X denoted broad gauge prior to the 1951 change to a W prefix letter.
17 November 1975

Our return from Agra was scheduled to go directly to Delhi Airport for a flight to Calcutta (Kolkata). However time gained allowed for spot of line side photography near Delhi. Class WP 4-6-2 No 7116, built 1964 at Chittaranjan works was seen heading the eastbound Delhi-Calcutta "Toofan Express". In later years its route was extended 340 miles to start at Sri Ganganagar, but the service ceased running in May 2020 after 91 years of operation. 17 November 1975

Calcutta, located in West Bengal was base for the group for one night and a single day, just enough time to visit the Eastern Railway MPD in the suburb of Howrah. On shed was another Class WP No 7589, but with a variation in the shape of a Giesl ejector. Although the loco was built by the Canadian Locomotive Company in 1956, the ejector wasn't fitted until circa 1967.
18 November 1975

Four Pacifics of Class XC, predecessors of the WP were present at Howrah. This example, No 22207, a 1928 product of Vulcan Foundry is in as built condition. Reports suggest they were top heavy and unstable at speed, thereby not at all liked by crews. Of the 72 XC's built, 40 came from Vulcan, with the remaining 32 coming from William Beardmore. After partition 50 remained in India the other 22 went to Pakistan.
18 November 1975

The Class XC had a propensity to suffer from cracked frames. In this view of No 22227, another 1928 built Vulcan Foundry example, the result of said fault is quite apparent with a pronounced droop in the firebox and cab area. Devoid of cow catcher and relegated to the role of shed pilot, the smoke deflectors fitted at some time in her past seem a bit superfluous to the old girl at this late stage in her life.
18 November 1975

As a British Engineering Standard Association (BESA) design, it would appear their team of designers were greatly influenced by the Great Central Railway Class J11 0-6-0. There is more than a passing resemblance of a J11 in this Class SGC 0-6-0 at Howrah. Built by North British in 1914 as a Class SG saturated locomotive, No 34181 was later superheated, becoming a <u>S</u>tandard <u>G</u>oods <u>C</u>onverted (SGC). Despite the Goods classification they frequently hauled passenger trains, albeit at low speed. Totalling 552, all were built in the UK by three companies. An odd point about these locomotives is the left hand exhaust steam pipe is on the outside, whilst on the right, it is inside, note the front end of a sister engine in the background.
18 November 1975

Ex Bengal & Nagpur Railway Class HSM 2-8-0 No 26184 was one of a batch of 47 locomotives built by Armstrong Whitworth in 1924. It is seen here clattering its way into Calcuttta Howrah terminus station with a parcels train. Locomotives of this batch perpetuated the design, as some had been built in 1914 by the Robert Stephenson Company.
18 November 1975

A Giesl fitted WP 4-6-2 No 7263 of the Eastern Railway makes a smoky exit from Howrah terminus as it gets a passenger train under way. This loco is one of the 300 built in 1949 in either Canada (200) or the USA (Baldwin 100), where positive builder identification is impossible due to early administration errors. Of note, just visible above the locomotive is one of the towers of the impressive Hoogly River, cantilever Road Bridge, often referred to as "The Gateway to Calcutta".
18 November 1975

The overnight 19.15 from Calcutta, Sealdah station to New Jalpaiguri is seen at Aluabari Road just after dawn in the hands of a Northeast Frontier Railway Class WP 4-6-2 No 7185. Built in 1965 at Chittaranjan, it exhibits spoked wheels as another minor design variation. No 7185 had taken over from Eastern Railway sister, No 7243 at some stage during the night. Both locomotives gave several group members fantastic footplate experiences during the hours of darkness. Note the three ladies and four children equipped with wicker baskets waiting patiently to sift through the ashes dropped from the firebox once the train departs. This practice of looking for partially burnt coal was a regular feature at way side stations in the days of steam in India.
19 November 1975

A 1943 built Alco 2-8-2 of Class MAWD, No 1764 brews up and blacks out the area as it shunts New Jalpaiguri yard. This locomotive is the Metre gauge version of the AWD/CWD classes nicknamed "Mac Arthurs" seen earlier. Three gauges of rails Broad, Metre and 2 foot were extant at New Jalpaiguri in 1975, a station that didn't exist 15 years earlier. A new Broad gauge line came to the area in 1960, which then continued eastward along a re-gauged metre gauge line. The truncated metre gauge track was realigned to terminate at New Jalpaiguri, whilst the Darjeeling Himalayan 2 foot gauge railway was extended 3 miles south east from Siliguri, allowing all three gauges to interchange.
19 November 1975

The Darjeeling Himalayan Railway (DHR) opened throughout in 1881 was to be the culmination of the TEFS tour, and what a culmination. Most had heard it was a spectacular railway, we were about to find out just how awe inspiring it was. Our motive power for the 55 mile, 8 hour trip was to be this 1925 built North British product. No 803, one of the celebrated Class B 0-4-0ST's, was just 16 months out of works, and was in tip top condition. Officially coal capacity is ¾ of a ton, there is a suspicion probably more is stacked in her bunker. This shot at the original DHR terminus shows the compact form and short wheel base of the B class, so ideally suited for the steep and tortuous DHR route.
19 November 1975

Two routes were added to the original DHR, to Kishanganj on the plains (1914), and the Teesta Valley line (1915), both were about 60-65 miles long. In 1914, primarily for the Kishanganj route, North British built two chunky Class C 4-6-2's, When, circa 1950, the route was converted to metre gauge the pair were virtually redundant as the Teesta Valley had been closed due washouts. This example, No 808, was noted outside New Jalpaiguri shed where a ban on photography was in place. Some of the group distracted the guides allowing others to grab a surreptitious picture, duplicates were duly forwarded later! Both locomotives survive plinthed, one No 807 in a Bombay museum and No 808 at the Northeast Frontier Railway headquarters.
19 November 1975

"Baby Sivok", this industrial 0-4-0WT was supplied by Orenstein & Koppel in 1913 for use building the DHR Kishanganj and Teesta Valley lines. Following which, it is believed to have been employed as shunter at the DHR Tindharia works until circa 1950. Then, to represent the DHR in Delhi for the 1953 centenary celebrations of Indian Railways, it was fitted with a false saddle tank and a plate dated 1881 (DHR opening year). From 1957 it was plinthed in Siliguri, as seen here, it returned to Tindharia in 1999, overhauled and steamed in 2000. It is now on display in a small museum at Ghum station, which at 7,407 feet is the summit of the DHR. Without the false saddle tank, it bears a strong resemblance to the Talyllyn Railway 0-4-0WT "Douglas".
21 November 1975

Invariably as the journey progressed up the DHR, many pictures were taken out of carriage windows. Following the three parts of the daily up train, our "special" basically formed a fourth section. It comprised a van containing our luggage and four coaches named after Himalayan mountains, in order, they were "Kanchenjunga", "Dhaulagiri", "Nanda Devi" with "Everest", an observation car on the rear. For most of the route the track ran adjacent to the Hill Cart Road, seen here in this view as gallant little No 803 forges up the line. During the ascent the railway criss-crosses the road 177 times to a cacophony of whistling. 19 November 1975

At Gayabari our train crossed the first of three sections of the daily down train, headed by Class B 0-4-0ST No 797. This engine was assembled at the DHR workshop Tindharia in 1925 using components supplied as "a kit of parts" by North British. In inclement weather when working in reverse the tarpaulin seen rolled and strapped to the cab roof is lowered to give basic protection. For completeness, on this day the other two down sections were headed by No 790 and No 799 respectively, whilst No's 792, 802 & 806 preceded our "special" going up.
19 November 1975

At the first Z reverse having caught up with the rear portion of the up service train we noticed passengers jumping off, running up to the next level and re-boarding. To paraphrase the saying, "When in India", at double Z reverses 2 and 3, we did likewise. Here No 803 having reversed up the section of track, visible lower left, now blasts up to the next reverse point from where it will propel in front of the red bush top centre and behind the buildings top left. The 4th and final reverse will take No 803 on its way to Tindharia. It is at one of the Z reverses that the maximum gradient on the DHR of 1 in 18/20, can be found. Some members of the group enjoy the splendours of the route from the roof of the train.
19 November 1975

Our intrepid cameraman Brian Walker, now joined his fellow travellers on the roof of the train. Not a sight seen on Settle & Carlisle line specials! In this view the chap on top of No 803 is the coal breaker/pusher, his job is to break up the large lumps of coal into manageable pieces and feed them down into the small bunker on the footplate, thereby making the fireman's job easier in the small cramped space available on the locomotive.
19 November 1975

The following day the group awoke in Darjeeling to find we had been blessed with a second day of glorious weather to enjoy the DHR. With a fleet of Land Rovers complete with Nepalese drivers at our disposal, we set off down the line. First stop was Batasia double spiral, here Brian Walker climbed to a higher view point to take in the complete loop. His fellow companions, seen centre, were taking the "cheesy shot" of a train with Himalayan peaks and the real Kanchenjunga in the background. Class B 0-4-0ST No 787 (North British 1913) having entered from the bottom left, begins its descent to Darjeeling, some 600ft below, with the 07.05 from Kurseong school train.
20 November 1975

Having followed all three sections of the down daily passenger service for about 30 miles, we encountered the first section of the up train. In this scene Class B, 0-4-0ST No 790 (North British 1914) at the head of section two is about to reverse into the refuge siding seen in the background, the guard gives the driver a green flag to proceed. Once No 799 had passed going downhill with the third and final part of the down service, No 790 continued to Darjeeling unimpeded... Alas to say, the forlorn figure on the road adjacent the 2nd coach is your humble caption writer!
20 November 1975

Having to wait for access into a congested Kurseong station is Class B 0-4-0ST No 804 (North British 1925) with the third portion of the up train. The two gentlemen on the front are the "sanding gear", in poor rail conditions they take sand from the hopper by their feet and sprinkle it on the track. The coal breaker and fireman are visible, as is one of the brakes men on the coach roof. This portion of the train was full of pupils from a girl's school, they too entered into the spirit of the chase, laughing, shouting and wildly gesticulating as we leapfrogged their train up the line. In this view as another Land Rover arrives, the girls "let rip" at the lads on board. All in all, the whole day was a marvellous, fun experience.
20 November 1975

Easing its way past the shops on the main street of Kurseong is Class B 0-4-0ST No 780 built by Sharp Stewart in 1892. It is heading the first section of the up train, having just taken over from No 797. Like the railway, Kurseong is built on the side of the Himalayan foothills, unable to go around the town, the railway has to go through it. In 1975 at least four up and four down steam hauled trains per day provided this sight, as a group we were privileged to experience the DHR in this unusual setting as a proper, hard working, narrow gauge steam railway. Now primarily diesel worked, steam usually only ventures out for tourists, in 1999 the DHR was classed as a UNESCO World Heritage Site.
20 November 1975

Just an hour before sunset, No 780 forges its way up toward Ghum and the summit of the line. In the foreground are some of the famed tiered Darjeeling tea plantations. In an area of high rain fall, the area is prone to landslides, what appears to be examples of soil stabilisation are visible on the slopes above the train. This 1892 built locomotive and its sister No 779 were the oldest working locomotives seen on the tour.
20 November 1975

A final photograph, on the final full day of scheduled activity for the group, fittingly taken on the "The Darj". By coincidence Class B 0-4-0ST, No 802 was the final locomotive delivered to the DHR coming from North British in 1927. It is seen in the forest not long after leaving Sukna with the first part of the daily up train. The group were en-route by road from Darjeeling to Bagdogra Airport for a flight to Bombay and eventually back to the UK. On hearing No 802 whistling and blasting its way toward us, the opportunity for just one more photograph on this incredible railway was too good to miss… So ended a magical, superb Indian Railway Experience.
21 November 1975